"The wound is the place where the Light enters you." – Rumi.

Healing your inner child is not just a journey into the past; it's a powerful step toward freeing your future. It's time to confront the shadows of your past and fully embrace the light of your present.

CLAIRE SAGY

The Hidden Shadow Self

A Journal Through Inner Child Healing

Copyright © 2024 by Claire Sagy

All rights reserved. No part of this publication may be reproduced, stored or transmitted in any form or by any means, electronic, mechanical, photocopying, recording, scanning, or otherwise without written permission from the publisher. It is illegal to copy this book, post it to a website, or distribute it by any other means without permission.

Claire Sagy asserts the moral right to be identified as the author of this work.

Claire Sagy has no responsibility for the persistence or accuracy of URLs for external or third-party Internet Websites referred to in this publication and does not guarantee that any content on such Websites is, or will remain, accurate or appropriate.

Designations used by companies to distinguish their products are often claimed as trademarks. All brand names and product names used in this book and on its cover are trade names, service marks, trademarks and registered trademarks of their respective owners. The publishers and the book are not associated with any product or vendor mentioned in this book. None of the companies referenced within the book have endorsed the book.

First edition

This book was professionally typeset on Reedsy. Find out more at reedsy.com

Contents

Prologue	1
Chapter 1	2
Chapter 2	12
Chapter 3	18
Chapter 4	27
Chapter 5	32
Chapter 6	40
Chapter 7	46
Chapter 8	51
References:	54
Also by Claire Sagy	56

Prologue

Medical Disclaimer:

The information provided in this journal is for educational and informational purposes only and is not intended as a substitute for professional medical advice, diagnosis, or treatment. Always seek the advice of your physician, therapist, or other qualified health provider with any questions you may have regarding a medical condition or mental health issue.

Although every effort has been made to ensure the accuracy of the information contained in this journal, the author and publisher assume no responsibility for errors or omissions or any consequences from the application of the information provided. The author and publisher shall not be held liable or responsible for any loss or damage allegedly arising from any information or suggestions contained within this journal.

Your use of the information in this journal is solely at your own risk. Always consult your healthcare provider for any health concerns you may have or might develop in the future.

Chapter 1

Welcome to your Shadow and Inner Child Journal!

Let me tell you that I am proud of you for taking matters into your own hands. The mere fact that you are willing to take a conscious look at your shadow is already healing you! You are fantastic, and I am proud of you! I wish you all the positive healing you can encounter in your inner child journey.

I find that doing my own shadow work helped me tremendously to overcome some basic personality deficits that I had lived with for decades.
   At first, I had sessions with a kinesiologist who introduced me to my shadow world. Later, I met with a healer who led me deeper into this world.

As a mum, I am trying to be super conscious of raising my children with as little shadow or inner child wound as possible. Since I have my own wounds and am far from perfect, I hope they will forgive me for those times when I failed them, causing them to work on their own shadow and inner child.

I hope this little booklet helps you in your life. It will give you

CHAPTER 1

tools to break free from old beliefs that others put on you so you can move forward in your spiritual journey. More importantly, it will help you notice when you've passed these beliefs down to your children and grandchildren.

Working on yourself is the first step to helping others. It's a lifelong journey, but it's essential so the next generation has fewer shadows to deal with. If we all do our part, we'll have fewer shadows to integrate, which will help us live up to our full potential. We can indeed be ourselves.

The only things that limit what we can achieve are our inner voice and beliefs. By working through our shadows, we can change this inner voice, realize our dreams, and feel whole again.

Claire

Hey, it's me, Claire.

Let me show you how one of my core beliefs formed at an early age:

Please keep in mind that this took place in the 70's.

I was almost five years old, and I had a baby brother. My mother was still a teenager when I was born.

One day, Mum had a doctor's appointment with my baby brother. Being so overwhelmed with the two little ones, she decided to leave me home alone while she took my baby brother to the doctor. My dad was in the army then so he couldn't help her.

My Mum told me that I was not allowed to open the door for anyone, that I had to be quiet and not scared, and that Mum would return soon.

Let's stop here. Telling a five-year-old not to be scared when you leave her alone at home just doesn't make sense. Of course, the child will feel extremely scared and anxious, and time will drag, and she will feel every minute, like an hour. It's irrational and irresponsible.

There was my Grandpa, who was an alcoholic. Therefore my Mum really hated him and didn't talk to him. But Grandpa loved me. I was his first grandchild.

So, while I am home alone, praying for my mum to be here right now so I wouldn't feel so alone and scared, Grandpa knocks on the door. (He probably saw Mum on the street and figured I must be home alone.)

At first, when my mum asked me to hide, I hid because I wanted to be a good girl. After all, she said I couldn't open the door to anybody. But this was my own grandpa, whom I also loved. Grandpa knew what to tell me. He spoke through the window and said if I came out, he would take me shopping and buy me nail polish!

Even though I was barely five years old, I loved all kinds of nail polish. However, my mum never let me have one, let alone use it. Besides, if I went with him, I wouldn't be alone anymore.

So I opened the door and went out with my Grandpa.

Mum came home, and the blood froze in her; as you can imagine, all kinds of images rushed through her mind: I went out alone, and a car hit me, somebody kidnapped me, all kind of horrible stuff, but anyway she will be in big trouble for sure, she might even have to go jail! You can imagine Mum's state of mind.

Then, soon, Grandpa brought me home. Even though he had a few drinks on the way, he still dearly loved me and took care of me. (And I got nail polish, too!)

CHAPTER 1

After my Mum had a loud fight with my Grandpa, she took out all her anger and frustration on me. She told me I was a useless girl because I didn't listen to her and opened the door. She called me a nasty girl because I caused so much anger and fear for her.

She projected her own fear onto me, making me responsible for her agony.

At the same time, I felt that I did the right thing because I was scared of being alone at home, and of course, I would go out with my grandpa, who I loved.

For a long time, she reminded me every day that this was all my fault. Whenever she asked me something, she reminded me to obey her and not be a bad girl like last time when she left me home alone.

This behavior reinforced my belief that I was responsible for her feelings. How others feel depends on my behavior. No wonder I have become a huge people-pleaser!

Of course, this wasn't the only time my Mum made me feel bad because of her feelings and emotional state.

As time passed, I started walking on eggshells and paying too much attention to ensure I didn't disappoint my Mum or others.

Slowly, I adopted this behavior, applying it to everyone, whether at work or in relationships. I started to behave like a slave; I even sacrificed my own needs above my partner's. I have lost myself and obeyed whatever my partner or boss wanted. This went on for years until I became exhausted and burnt out.

That's when I started doing shadow work. I directed my attention inward and began to change.

Now, look at the definition of:

Codependency and Emotional Enmeshment:

Codependency often develops in individuals who, as children, were placed in a role where they had to take care of or manage the emotions of their caregivers. These children learn to derive their sense of worth from being needed and often suppress their own needs to maintain harmony.

- **As Adults:**
- Codependent individuals may seek out relationships where they can "rescue" or care for others, often at the expense of their well-being. They may struggle to set boundaries and feel responsible for their partner's happiness, leading to emotional enmeshment—where their identity becomes so intertwined with their partner's that they lose sight of their own needs and desires. This can create an unbalanced relationship dynamic, where the codependent person may feel resentful, exhausted, or unappreciated yet unable to break free from the cycle of caretaking.

This was absolutely me. I have denied myself for the sake of others.

But let's not run ahead too much. I want to explain the basics of Shadow work and Inner child work—the practices where you can bring up these buried emotions and little stories and snippets that determine your personality by the time you have grown up.

You can also have a journal at hand if you want. Use them to jot down the memories that will pop up while reading this book—just the essence of it, so you won't forget it. Later, you can elaborate on them.

CHAPTER 1

The Concept of the Inner Child

The inner child echoes your childhood self, carrying the memories, emotions, and beliefs you formed during those early years. It represents both the innocent, playful aspects of your personality and the vulnerable parts that may have experienced hurt or neglect. When we talk about "inner child work," we're referring to the process of reconnecting with this part of ourselves, understanding its needs, and healing any wounds that have been carried into adulthood. The experiences and messages we absorb in childhood lay the foundation for how we see ourselves as adults. When those experiences are negative or traumatic, they can lead to deep-seated feelings of unworthiness or inadequacy.

Especially as young children, we need lots of love, nurturing, soothing, and feeling needed and cared for. When we do not receive these throughout our lives, we get them from elsewhere, anywhere from outside. For example, that's the main reason people are developing different kinds of addictions. Not just addiction to substances can be addiction from being in love, resulting in chasing relationships, sex addiction, or addiction from acceptance at the workplace or within our circle. Etc.

However, through inner child and shadow work, we can heal these wounds, transform negative beliefs, and develop a healthier, more compassionate relationship with ourselves.

Why We Lose Touch with Our Inner Child

As we grow up, societal expectations, responsibilities, and life experiences often lead us to suppress our inner child. We learn to prioritize logic over emotion, productivity overplay, and independence over vulnerability. While these traits are necessary for functioning in the adult world, they can also cause us to lose touch with the parts of ourselves that need care and attention. Over time, this disconnection can manifest as emotional imbalances, unresolved trauma, and a sense of emptiness. That's where shadow work comes in—connecting ourselves back to our child self.

What is the Shadow self?

The shadow self represents the parts of our personality that we hide or suppress because they are considered undesirable by ourselves, our families, or society. These aspects of our personality are not inherently negative. Still, they become part of the shadow because they are deemed unacceptable by the people and environments that shape us, particularly during our formative years.

Examples of Shadow Aspects:

These repressed parts can include a wide range of traits or emotions, such as anger, sadness, jealousy, sexuality, creativity, assertiveness, or even certain desires and ambitions. For example, a child who is told that showing anger is bad might suppress their natural feelings of anger, pushing it into their shadow. Similarly, a child who is overly criticized for being sensitive might start to hide their vulnerability.

What is Shadow Work?

Shadow work is a term coined by psychologist Carl Jung. It refers to the process of exploring the unconscious parts of our personality—the "shadow self." This shadow consists of the traits, emotions, and experiences we have repressed or denied, often because they were deemed unacceptable or too painful to face. Shadow work involves bringing these hidden aspects to light, acknowledging them, and integrating them into our conscious selves. It's not always easy, but it's a crucial step in healing and personal growth.

The Connection Between Shadow Work and the Inner Child

Our inner child often resides in the shadow, hidden away because its needs are unmet or its emotions are too overwhelming. By engaging in shadow work, we can uncover these buried parts of ourselves, allowing us to reconnect with our inner child. This connection is essential for healing past wounds and developing a more authentic, balanced sense of self. It's like finding a lost puzzle piece that makes the whole picture clearer and more complete.

Children are incredibly vulnerable, their survival entirely dependent on the care and protection of their parents. Because of this dependence, they often endure whatever treatment comes their way, whether it's love or neglect, kindness or abuse. With no other choice, they accept and adapt to their circumstances, no matter how painful or damaging. By adopting, I mean exactly that: they learn to suppress emotions and needs based on what kind of care they receive, especially in their early life.

When a child is neglected or mistreated, the impact is profound and lasting. Growing up without love or with abusive parents can harden their hearts, leaving them with little empathy or compassion for others. They learn early on that they cannot rely on anyone to meet their needs, making it difficult for them to connect with others or feel genuine concern for anyone else's well-being. They were told that their needs didn't matter or their feelings were not that important to their parents, so when they grew up, they would treat themselves and others in the same way, too. They will not feel empathy or compassion towards someone else's situation because when they needed empathy, they did not receive it—just a tiny example. You finally had your ice cream as a child or a candy floss, and you dropped it…you felt like your whole world collapsed, but your parents said, Oh, it's just an ice cream! Don't cry for it! It's a tiny, simple example of how something significant for you meant nothing for someone else.

How their parents treated them shapes their view of the world, often leading them to believe that indifference or cruelty is the norm. In this way, the cycle of neglect and emotional distance continues, passed down from generation to generation.

Healing Through Inner Child and Shadow Work

Healing from these early wounds involves reconnecting with the inner child, acknowledging the shadow self, and rewriting the negative core beliefs formed in childhood.

Reparenting the Inner Child: Inner child work often involves "reparenting" yourself—offering the love, validation, and care your inner child needed but didn't receive. This process helps to heal the wounds of the past and build a stronger, more positive self-image. When you are dealing with a childhood memory while you remember it, you can "change" it by imagining your present self going there and comforting your child self, cuddling, cherishing, talking softly to him/her,

CHAPTER 1

and giving her/him the understanding love what was missing in the given situation. Rewrite the scene of your memory. You bring it to the light through this positive care, and your mind won't suppress it anymore; it will become neutral instead of a negative, hurtful memory.

You might want to have a packet of tissues handy. These memories could bring up extreme emotions, and don't forget that they were buried for years. They are powerful.

Chapter 2

How does the Shadow Self develop?

Development of the shadow self begins in childhood, as we learn what behaviors and traits are rewarded and which are punished or frowned upon.

Parents, teachers, and society play a significant role in shaping our shadow. For instance, a boy might be told that "boys don't cry," leading him to suppress his sadness and vulnerability. A girl might be encouraged to be "nice" and "polite," causing her to suppress her anger or assertiveness. Over time, these repressed parts become unconscious, forming what Jung calls the shadow self.

Cultural norms and gender expectations also heavily influence what we suppress. Certain cultures value stoicism (the endurance of pain or hardship without displaying feelings and complaints) over emotional expression, leading people to repress their emotions. Gender norms might dictate that women should be nurturing and men should be strong, causing individuals to repress traits that don't align with these stereotypes.

Social Learning Theory, developed by psychologist Albert Bandura, posits that much human behavior is learned through observation and imitation rather than direct instruction or trial and error. This theory emphasizes the significant role of the environment, particularly caregivers and other influential figures, in shaping a child's behavior, attitudes, and beliefs. That's exactly when you tell your child not to swear, but you swear, so do they, rather than listening to what you said. Or when you tell them not to smoke when they grow up, but you smoke all the time. Can you see the pattern here? This is called a generational pattern. We aim to break it. You are on your way to break it by just willing to work on yourself. Well done!

Social learning theory suggests that children learn through their own experiences and by observing the actions, attitudes, and outcomes of others' behaviors. This learning process is called "modeling," where the child watches and then imitates the behaviors and emotional responses of those around them.

Modeling Behavior: How Children Learn Through Observation

Children are like sponges, absorbing the behaviors, attitudes, and emotional reactions of the people they observe regularly, especially those they view as role models—typically their parents, guardians, or teachers. This theory suggests that much of human learning occurs in a social context, where behaviors are shaped not just by direct experience but also by watching others and the consequences of their actions.

1. Imitation of Caregiver Behavior:
Adopting Self-Critical Behaviors:

If a child consistently observes a parent or caregiver engaging in self-critical behavior—such as making negative comments about their appearance, doubting their abilities, or expressing feelings of inadequacy—the child will likely internalize these behaviors. For example, if a mother frequently says, "I'm so fat" or "I'm terrible at this," the child may learn to mirror this self-critical language and adopt similar attitudes toward their body or capabilities. This modeling of behavior teaches the child that it's normal or expected to be self-critical, laying the groundwork for a negative self-image and low self-esteem.

Inheriting Self-Defeating Attitudes:

In addition to specific behaviors, children also absorb general attitudes and beliefs about the world. If a child's caregivers consistently exhibit self-defeating attitudes—such as believing they will never succeed or are undeserving of happiness— the child may adopt these same pessimistic views. This can manifest in adulthood as a tendency to self-sabotage, avoid taking risks, or settle for less than they deserve because they've learned to expect failure or disappointment.

2. The Role of Reinforcement and Punishment:

Reinforcement and punishment also play crucial roles in social learning. Children observe how certain behaviors are rewarded or punished in their environment and use this information to guide their actions.

Positive Reinforcement:

Suppose a child observes that a parent receives praise or affection after demonstrating a particular behavior, such as showing kindness or achieving something at work. In that case, the child will likely imitate that behavior to receive similar positive reinforcement. This is how positive traits like generosity, perseverance, and kindness can be passed down.

Negative Reinforcement and Punishment:

Conversely, suppose a child sees a parent being harshly critical of themselves and receiving no correction or even being encouraged (perhaps by another adult who also models self-criticism). In that case, the child might learn that self-criticism is acceptable or expected. Similarly, suppose a child's attempts to express themselves are met with punishment or disapproval. In that case, they may learn to suppress their thoughts and emotions to avoid negative consequences, leading to issues like low self-esteem or fear of failure in the future.

3. Observing Emotional Management:

Children learn behaviors from their caregivers and how to manage and express their emotions. How adults handle their feelings provides a powerful template for children, who often mimic these emotional responses.

Healthy Emotional Expression:

If children observe their parents healthily managing emotions—acknowledging feelings, discussing them openly, and working through them constructively—they are more likely to develop similar skills. For example, if a parent calmly discusses their frustration and finds a solution, the child learns that it's okay to feel frustrated and that there are constructive ways to handle it.

Unhealthy Emotional Responses:

On the other hand, if a parent frequently suppresses their emotions, lashes out in anger, or exhibits anxiety without discussing it, the child may learn to either mimic these unhealthy responses or become emotionally repressed. For instance, a child who sees a parent constantly bottling up anger might learn to do the same, believing that anger is dangerous or unacceptable. This can lead to emotional repression, where the child grows up feeling unable or unwilling to express certain emotions, potentially leading to issues like anxiety, depression, or chronic stress in adulthood.

4. Validation (or Invalidation) of Emotions:

Validation of emotions is crucial in developing a healthy sense of self. Children rely on their caregivers not just for physical care but also for emotional guidance. When a child's emotions are validated, they learn that their feelings are legitimate and vital, contributing to a positive self-image.

Positive Validation:

If a child expresses sadness or fear and is met with empathy and understanding, they learn that their emotions are valid and that it's okay to feel and express them. For example, if a child is upset after a bad day at school and their parent listens and offers comfort, they learn that their emotions matter and that seeking support is a healthy response to emotional distress. This validation helps the child develop emotional intelligence and resilience.

Emotional Invalidation:

Conversely, if a child's emotions are consistently dismissed or invalidated—such as being told, "Stop crying, it's not a big deal," or "You're being too sensitive"—they may learn that their feelings are unimportant or wrong. This can lead to emotional repression, where the child grows up believing that expressing their feelings is inappropriate or that they should always present a "tough" or indifferent exterior. Over time, this can contribute to a diminished sense of self-worth as the child learns to prioritize the emotions and expectations of others over their own.

(How often have we been told, ' Don't cry, or else I'll give you something to cry about!'? That's even more threatening. We feel like we have to hold back our emotions. Otherwise, the parents will get physical and hurt us. It's unbelievable! But see how far we have come already. At least we recognize how harmful this is, talk about it, and try not to follow this harmful behavior from now on so our children won't suffer the same way as we do.)

5. Long-Term Effects of Emotional Invalidation:

The long-term effects of emotional invalidation can be profound. When children grow up in an environment where their emotions are consistently dismissed, they may struggle with identifying and expressing their feelings as adults. They might also develop a fear of vulnerability, as they've learned that showing emotions can lead to rejection or ridicule.

Emotional Repression:

Emotional repression often leads to a lack of self-awareness, as the individual disconnects from their emotional experiences. This can manifest as difficulty forming deep, meaningful relationships and managing stress or navigating complex emotional situations. The person may also experience chronic anxiety or depression because their emotional needs are not being met, and they have not developed healthy ways to process or express their feelings.

Diminished Sense of Self:

A diminished sense of self often accompanies emotional repression. When children learn their emotions are invalid, they may start to believe that they are unimportant or that their needs and desires don't matter. This can lead to a pattern of self-neglect, where the individual prioritizes others' needs over their own, or it can result in a lack of confidence and difficulty in asserting themselves in personal and professional situations.

Chapter 3

How can you remember?

Remembering childhood memories, especially those that are deeply buried or associated with trauma, can be challenging. However, various methods and techniques can help individuals access these memories and bring them to the surface. Feel free to experiment with this method. Since you have chosen this book, you will likely already practice one or more. You do not have to run to a therapist; if you want, you can make this process free. However, a trained professional can speed up this process and hold space for you simultaneously. A good friend can also hold space for you if you are confined in them.

1. Journaling

Stream-of-Consciousness Writing: This technique involves writing continuously without worrying about grammar, spelling, or structure. The goal is to let thoughts flow freely onto the page. By doing this regularly, you might find that old memories, emotions, and experiences start to surface, often unexpectedly.

    Prompted Journaling: Use the lined page of this workbook and answer the questions.

Just Plain Journaling: When these buried memories come up, they can often be faint or patchy. Sometimes, you can't remember the whole situation, just bits. It is helpful to write down those because they are so "new" you can easily forget them. Also, writing them down helps them return to your conscious memory, and you can recall the whole story.

Trigger Identification: Notice what triggers strong emotions in your daily life. These triggers often point to unresolved issues from your past, which can lead you to your inner child or shadow self.

2. Meditation and Mindfulness

Mindfulness Meditation: Practicing mindfulness involves focusing on the present moment without judgment. Memories may surface naturally as you become more attuned to your thoughts and feelings. This process can be enhanced by focusing on sensations or emotions that arise during meditation and gently exploring them. Meditation is the most common practice. It is fundamental to quiet your mind and gain control over your thoughts so they do not control you. Many meditation apps are available, YouTube has even more variation, and books are teaching you this practice. Whether you do it as a pro or a beginner, it will help you advance your self-discovery journey. It is better to do it imperfectly than not meditating at all. If that helps, there are groups online on Facebook, Eventbrite, and other social media where you can participate in group meditation (guided or not guided) for free. That can hold you accountable for showing up if you struggle to start.

Guided Imagery Meditation: This technique involves listening to a guided meditation that takes you back to your childhood environment. For example, a guide might ask you to visualize your childhood home, school, or event. As you engage with these visualizations, suppressed memories may begin to emerge. Write them down and turn them into a positive memory by attending to your child-self.

Inner Child Meditation: Practice guided meditations to connect with your inner child. These meditations often involve visualizing your younger self and offering them love, comfort, and understanding.

3. Practice Mindfulness and Self-Compassion

Mindfulness: Engage in mindfulness practices to become more aware of your thoughts, emotions, and behaviors. Mindfulness helps you observe these without judgment, making uncovering hidden aspects of yourself more accessible.

What is mindfulness?: Mindfulness is the practice of paying attention to the present moment non-judgmentally. It involves being fully aware of your thoughts, feelings, sensations, and environment without trying to change or judge them.

Self-Compassion: Cultivate a compassionate attitude towards yourself as you engage in this work. Remember that the goal is not to criticize or judge yourself but to understand and heal.

4. Start Small and Be Patient

Small Steps: Begin with small, manageable steps, like journaling for a few minutes each day or doing a short meditation.

Don't rush the process; deep healing takes time.

Patience: Be patient with yourself. Inner child and shadow work can bring up intense emotions and memories. It is important to allow yourself the time and space to process these experiences.

5. Therapy

Talk Therapy: Speaking with a therapist can create a safe space for memories to surface. Therapists often use specific questioning techniques to explore childhood experiences, helping clients connect the dots between their past and present feelings or behaviors.

Cognitive-behavioral therapy (CBT) can help you identify and challenge negative beliefs formed in childhood. While CBT focuses on present thoughts and behaviors, it often leads to discussions about past experiences, which can trigger the recall of related memories.

Psychodynamic Therapy: This approach delves into unconscious processes and past experiences that shape current behavior. It's particularly effective in uncovering repressed memories and exploring the impact of early childhood on present life.

Eye Movement Desensitization and Reprocessing (EMDR): Originally developed to treat trauma, EMDR uses specific eye movements or other forms of bilateral stimulation to help people process traumatic memories. As these memories are processed, other related memories, including childhood ones, may also surface.

Kinesiology: It's a non-invasive practice that works with your body's natural healing abilities. Kinesiology is a therapeutic practice that taps into the body's natural ability to heal itself. Unlike traditional therapy, which often focuses on talking through issues, kinesiology uses muscle testing to directly access the body's subconscious directly, identifying issues that may not be consciously recognized. Kinesiology can also be incredibly effective in inner child work. Accessing subconscious memories and emotions helps you reconnect with your inner child, uncovering what needs to be healed. Helping you access and release deeply held emotions can pave the way for profound personal transformation. I am personally a big fan of kinesiology. I had lots of a-ha moments while I was in the sessions. I have to warn you, though: I had more past life memories surface than these life memories. You might want to tell your practitioner in advance if you want to focus solely on this life.

6. Hypnotherapy

Hypnosis: A trained hypnotherapist can guide you into deep relaxation where your conscious mind becomes less dominant, allowing access to the subconscious mind. In this state, repressed memories from childhood may become more accessible. Hypnotherapy can be beneficial for uncovering memories that are too painful or difficult to recall consciously. I strongly advise you against hypnosis if you are at the beginning of your self-discovery journey. The memories coming up to the surface can shock you. Not everyone can handle them.

7. Creative Arts

Art Therapy: Engaging in creative activities like drawing, painting, or sculpting can help access subconscious memories. For example, you might be asked to draw your childhood home or a significant event from your past. Creating art can bypass the logical mind, allowing repressed memories to surface in symbolic forms.

Music Therapy: Listening to or creating music, especially songs from your childhood, can evoke strong emotional responses and trigger memories. Music uniquely connects us to our past, often bringing forgotten experiences to the surface.

Writing Fiction or Poetry: Sometimes, writing stories or poems loosely based on your own life can help you access childhood memories. The creative process allows you to explore emotions and experiences from different angles, often revealing hidden aspects of your past.

8. Dream Analysis

Dream Journaling: Keep a journal by your bedside and write down your dreams immediately upon waking. Dreams often contain symbols and narratives related to unresolved issues from childhood. You might uncover memories buried in your subconscious by analyzing these dreams, either on your own or with a therapist.

Lucid Dreaming: This technique involves becoming aware that you are dreaming while still in the dream state. With practice, you can use lucid dreaming to explore your subconscious mind and potentially access repressed memories. However, it is not for everyone.

9. Sensory Triggers

Scent: Certain smells, like the scent of a particular food, perfume, or environment, can trigger memories from childhood. For instance, the smell of your mother's perfume might bring back memories of being held by her as a child.

Taste: Tasting foods that were significant during your childhood, like a favorite dessert or meal, can evoke strong memories associated with those tastes.

Touch: Physical sensations, like touching an old toy or sitting in a familiar environment, can bring back tactile memories from your childhood.

Photographs and Objects: Looking at old family photos, toys, or objects from your childhood can trigger memories and help you reconnect with past experiences.

10. Movement and Body Awareness

Body Scanning: This technique involves paying close attention to the sensations in different parts of your body. Often, memories are stored in the body, and by focusing on physical sensations, you may trigger the recall of associated memories. For example, tension in your shoulders might be linked to a childhood memory of feeling burdened or stressed. You can utilize guided meditation for this if you like.

Somatic Experiencing: Developed by Dr. Peter Levine, this therapeutic approach focuses on the body's physical sensations to release trauma. By tuning into the body, individuals can access and process memories stored in the body's tissues, which might not be accessible through verbal therapy alone.

11. Regression Techniques

Age Regression Therapy is a specialized form of therapy in which the therapist guides you back to earlier stages of your life, helping you re-experience and process memories from your childhood. This technique can be done through hypnosis or other therapeutic methods and can be particularly effective in accessing repressed or forgotten memories.

Past Life Regression: Though more controversial and less scientifically validated, some people find that exploring past lives (whether real or symbolic) through regression can bring up memories metaphorically related to unresolved childhood issues. This can result in severe side effects.

12. Group Therapy and Support Groups

Shared Experiences: Engaging in group therapy or support groups where participants share their childhood experiences can trigger your own memories. Hearing others talk about their childhood can spark similar memories in you, bringing long-forgotten experiences to the surface.

Safe Space for Exploration: A supportive group environment can provide a sense of safety and community, which may encourage the surfacing of previously too difficult memories to face alone.

13. Integrate What You Learn

Application in Daily Life: As you uncover aspects of your inner child and shadow, look for ways to integrate these insights into your daily life. This could involve setting boundaries, expressing your needs, or practicing self-care.

Continuous Practice: Inner child and shadow work is not a one-time event but a constant practice. Regularly revisit these exercises and reflections to deepen your understanding and healing.

14. Accept and Embrace All Parts of Yourself

Non-Judgmental Acceptance: The ultimate goal of inner child and shadow work is to accept and integrate all parts of yourself, including the parts you may have been ashamed of or afraid to acknowledge. Embrace your whole self with compassion and love.

Conclusion:

Please use these therapies at your own risk. Research before you choose a therapy. Not all of them are suitable for everyone. There is a reason why your body puts these memories in the shadows. Bringing them up can bring up physical pain, which can persist in your life if not treated by a professional.

Chapter 4

Examples of other people

Example 1: Overcoming Fear of Rejection

Scenario:
Beatrice, a 32-year-old professional, has always struggled with the fear of rejection. Whether in her relationships or at work, she avoids situations where she might face criticism or be turned down. This fear has held her back from pursuing promotions, sharing her ideas in meetings, and even forming deep connections with others.

Inner Child Work:
Beatrice decided to explore inner child work to understand the root of her fear. Through journaling and guided meditations, she recalled a memory from her childhood where a parent repeatedly criticized her for not meeting high expectations. This constant criticism left her feeling inadequate and afraid of making mistakes.

By visualizing her younger self, Beatrice began to comfort her inner child, acknowledging the pain and fear she had felt back then. She reassured her inner child that it's okay to make mistakes and that others' approval doesn't define her worth. Over time, this practice helped Beatrice build self-compassion and reduce her fear of rejection. She started to take small risks at work, like sharing her ideas more openly and noticed a positive shift in her confidence and relationships.

Example 2: Healing Anger Issues

Scenario:

Peter, a 40-year-old father, often loses his temper over minor things, especially with his kids. He knows his anger is disproportionate to the situation, but he feels powerless to control it. This ongoing issue is straining his relationship with his family and causing him a lot of guilt.

Shadow Work:

Peter decided to engage in shadow work to uncover the deeper cause of his anger. Through therapy and self-reflection, he discovered that his anger was rooted in unresolved feelings of powerlessness from his childhood. Growing up, Peter had an authoritarian father who frequently belittled him, and as a child, he felt helpless to defend himself.

These repressed feelings of helplessness had manifested as anger in his adult life, particularly in situations where he felt out of control. By acknowledging this shadow aspect of himself—the part that felt weak and unheard—Peter could start the healing process. He practiced mindfulness to observe his anger without acting on it and learned to express his needs healthily. Over time, his outbursts became less frequent, and his relationship with his children improved as he modeled better emotional regulation.

Example 3: Letting Go of Perfectionism

Scenario:

Summer, a 28-year-old artist, has always struggled with perfectionism. She often spends hours reworking her paintings, never feeling satisfied with the final product. This perfectionism also spills over into other areas of her life, causing stress and anxiety.

Inner Child and Shadow Work:

Summer began exploring the roots of her perfectionism through inner child work and shadow work. She remembered how, as a child, she was often praised for her achievements but criticized for any mistakes. This created a belief that her worth was tied to being perfect, and she developed a fear of failure.

In her shadow work, Summer uncovered a part of herself that was deeply afraid of being seen as "not good enough." This shadow aspect drove her perfectionism, keeping her in a self-criticism cycle. Through inner child work, she visualized comforting her younger self, reminding her that it's okay to be imperfect and that mistakes are part of the creative process.

Summer gradually let go of the need for perfection as she integrated these insights. She started to embrace her artistic process, accepting that not every piece needed to be flawless. This shift allowed her to create more freely and reduced the stress she had been carrying for years.

Example 4: Releasing Guilt and Shame

Scenario:

Mona, a 45-year-old nurse, has always felt deep guilt and shame, particularly when setting boundaries. She often says "yes" to requests, even when exhausted, and finds it challenging to prioritize her needs. This pattern has led to burnout and resentment, but she feels too guilty to change it.

Shadow Work:

Mona decided to delve into shadow work to understand why she struggled so much with guilt and shame. Through introspection and therapy, she uncovered a childhood memory where she was made to feel responsible for her parents' happiness. She was told she was selfish whenever she asserted her own needs, which planted the seeds of guilt and shame.

In her shadow work, Mona faced the deeply ingrained belief that her needs were less important than others. By acknowledging this shadow part of herself—the part that felt unworthy of self-care—she began to challenge and reframe these beliefs. Lisa practiced setting small boundaries and, despite initial discomfort, realized that the world didn't fall apart when she said "no."

As she continued this work, the grip of guilt and shame loosened, allowing Mona to care for herself without the overwhelming sense of obligation. This change led to a healthier work-life balance and a more fulfilling personal life.

Example 5: Addressing Relationship Patterns

Scenario:

A 38-year-old software engineer, Will has noticed a recurring pattern in his romantic relationships. He often feels overly dependent on his partners for emotional validation and struggles with intense jealousy, which has led to the breakdown of several relationships.

Inner Child Work:

CHAPTER 4

Will began inner child work to understand the roots of his dependency and jealousy. Through meditation and guided imagery, he connected with his inner child, who had felt neglected and emotionally abandoned by his parents during his formative years. This childhood experience created a deep-seated fear of abandonment, which was playing out in his adult relationships.

By reconnecting with his inner child, Will learned to provide the love and reassurance his younger self had been missing. He practiced affirmations and visualization exercises to build a sense of security within himself rather than seeking it solely from others. Over time, this inner work reduced his jealousy and dependency, allowing him to form healthier, more balanced relationships.

Chapter 5

Attachment Styles in Relationships

Insecure Attachment and Its Impact on Relationships:

Attachment styles, formed during childhood, continue to shape how we connect with others in adulthood. These styles—secure, anxious, avoidant, and disorganized—can profoundly influence the dynamics of our relationships.

Anxious Attachment:

Individuals with an anxious attachment style often crave closeness and intimacy but simultaneously fear that their partner will abandon or reject them. This fear stems from inconsistent or unpredictable caregiving in childhood, where the child learns that love and attention might be withdrawn at any moment. As adults, these individuals may become overly dependent on their partners, needing constant reassurance and validation. They might also experience intense jealousy, constantly worried that their partner is losing interest or being unfaithful, even when there's no evidence to support these fears. This anxiety can lead to clingy behaviors, such as excessive texting or calling or being overly possessive, which can strain the relationship.

For example, the alcoholic parents' attention towards their children often changes depending on their level of soberness. They either love or neglect their children's emotions, not having enough capacity to deal with their children's feelings when they are intoxicated.

Avoidant Attachment:

Those with an avoidant attachment style often struggle with intimacy and emotional closeness. This style typically develops when a child's emotional needs are consistently ignored or minimized, leading them to believe that depending on others is unsafe. As adults, they may prioritize independence to an extreme degree, avoiding vulnerability and keeping their partners at a distance. They might be uncomfortable with emotional expressions and may withdraw from partners when they feel overwhelmed. This can lead to a lack of deep connection in relationships, as avoidant individuals may find it challenging to fully open up or commit, often leading to emotional withdrawal and the perception that they are "unavailable" or "cold."

This can trigger the abandonment wound for these people's partners. When this type of partner withdraws, the other partner may have a similar experience when they have been abandoned by their parents, for example, when the parents are divorced or die. This unconsciously makes them feel rejected or unwanted, and that can lead to an argument or fight in the relationship, which eventually will decay the relationship itself.

Disorganized Attachment:

Disorganized attachment is often the result of childhood

trauma, such as abuse or neglect, where the caregiver is both a source of comfort and fear. This creates a conflicting dynamic where the child doesn't know whether to approach or avoid the caregiver. This can manifest as a push-pull dynamic in adult relationships, where the individual oscillates between wanting closeness and pushing their partner away. They may have difficulty trusting others and exhibit erratic or unpredictable relationship behavior. This can lead to turbulent relationships as the person struggles with conflicting desires for connection and self-protection.

There is Matthew. His dad was usually a very typical father. From the point of view of the outsider, he looked like a loving father. He was a drummer in a band, just as a hobby, but when he wanted to punish Matthew, he took out his drumsticks, made Matthew lie on the bed on his belly, and beat him up with his drumstick, hitting Matthew's bottom. This hasn't occurred often, but it always kept Matthew on edge when approaching his father—a typical example of a disorganized attachment. Matthew is my brother. He still can't forgive our father, and I don't blame him. He is dealing with his shadow.

Codependency and Emotional Enmeshment:

Codependency often develops in individuals who, as children, were placed in a role where they had to take care of or manage the emotions of their caregivers. These children learn to derive their sense of worth from being needed and often suppress their own needs to maintain harmony.

As Adults:
Codependent individuals may seek out relationships where

they can "rescue" or care for others, often at the expense of their well-being. They may struggle to set boundaries and feel responsible for their partner's happiness, leading to emotional enmeshment—where their identity becomes so intertwined with their partner's that they lose sight of their own needs and desires. This can create an unbalanced relationship dynamic, where the codependent person may feel resentful, exhausted, or unappreciated, yet unable to break free from the cycle of caretaking.

Avoidance and Sabotage

Self-Sabotage in Relationships:
Self-sabotage occurs when individuals unconsciously undermine their own happiness or success, often because, deep down, they believe they don't deserve it. This behavior is typically rooted in negative core beliefs formed in childhood, such as "I am not good enough," "I am unlovable," or "I will always be abandoned."

Someone who feels unworthy of love may unconsciously push their partner away to avoid the risk of being rejected. For instance, they might pick fights over trivial matters, become distant, or even cheat, creating a scenario where the relationship is likely to fail. This behavior is often a defense mechanism to avoid the pain of potential rejection; ending the relationship on their terms gives them a sense of control. Unfortunately, this creates a self-fulfilling prophecy, reinforcing their belief that they are unlovable or that all relationships end in heartbreak. This cycle can be difficult to break because each failure or rejection serves as "proof" of the individual's negative beliefs about themselves. They might say things like, "See, I knew I wasn't good enough," or "This always happens to me," further entrenching these damaging beliefs.

Avoidance of Intimacy and Success:

Avoidance is another typical response to deep-seated feelings of inadequacy. If a person believes they are unworthy of success, love, or happiness, they might avoid situations where they could achieve these things, fearing that they will ultimately fail or be exposed as a fraud.

Individuals might avoid applying for promotions or taking on new challenges at work because they fear they won't measure up or don't truly deserve success. This can lead to a stagnant career and reinforce feelings of inadequacy. In personal relationships, they might avoid deep emotional connections or commitment because they are afraid of being vulnerable or hurt. They might keep relationships at a surface level, avoid talking about feelings, or shy away from making long-term plans, preventing them from experiencing love and intimacy.

Fear of Happiness:

Some people may have an unconscious fear of happiness, known as cherophobia. This fear can stem from believing that happiness is fleeting or will be followed by negative consequences. For example, if a person experiences trauma or loss after a period of happiness in childhood, they might associate happiness with impending doom.

Such individuals might struggle to fully enjoy or trust in happy moments, constantly waiting for "the other shoe to drop." This can lead them to avoid situations that could bring joy or downplay positive experiences. In relationships, they might sabotage good moments by starting arguments or creating distance because, deep down, they fear that happiness is too good to last.

Impact on Self-Image and Perpetuation of Negative Cycles

When we repress certain qualities, they don't just disappear—they remain in the unconscious and can manifest in various ways, often negatively impacting our lives. These deeply ingrained behavior patterns can be challenging to change because they are often unconscious. Many people are unaware of how their childhood experiences influence relationships and behaviors. They may repeat the same patterns without this awareness, even when they want to change.

When we repress certain qualities, they don't just disappear—they remain in the unconscious and can manifest in various ways, often negatively impacting our lives. Some can carry this hurt for decades.

Repressed qualities usually resurface as feelings of inadequacy, guilt, or shame. For example, if you've repressed your assertiveness because it was discouraged in childhood, you might feel inadequate or guilty when you try to stand up for yourself as an adult. These feelings can undermine your self-confidence and lead to a pattern of self-sabotage or passive-aggressive behavior.

Disconnection from the True Self

The more we repress significant parts of ourselves, the more disconnected we become from our true selves. This disconnection can lead to a range of psychological and emotional issues.

When we deny parts of ourselves, we essentially deny our

wholeness. This can lead to a persistent feeling of incompleteness or emptiness. You might feel like something is missing in your life, or you're not meeting your expectations, even if you can't pinpoint why.

Disconnection from your true self can also fuel low self-esteem. Developing a healthy, positive self-image is challenging if you constantly reject parts of yourself. This internal conflict between who you are and who you feel you're allowed to be can create a deep sense of unworthiness or self-doubt.

Over time, if we continue to suppress our shadow, we might start living according to a "false self"—a persona created to fit the expectations of others rather than expressing our true desires, feelings, and needs. This can lead to a life that feels inauthentic, where you're constantly trying to conform to what you believe others expect of you rather than living in alignment with your true nature. When this gets serious and not dealt with, it manifests as physical symptoms and illness.

The Process of Integration

Shadow work requires a conscious effort to explore the darker aspects of your personality. The goal of shadow work is to bring these repressed parts of the self into the light of consciousness and integrate them into our whole being. As you engage in shadow work and reconnect with your inner child, you may uncover past traumas that need healing. It's essential to approach these memories with compassion and allow yourself to feel and release the emotions. This process can be challenging but essential for healing and growth.

The first step is acknowledging and accepting these repressed parts without judgment. This means recognizing that emotions like shame or traits like assertiveness are not inherently wrong—they are natural parts of the human experience.

Once you've acknowledged and explored your shadow, the next step is to integrate these parts into your conscious self. This might involve expressing repressed emotions in healthy ways, embracing traits you once considered undesirable, and allowing yourself to be fully who you are. Integrating your shadow allows you to live more authentically and feel more complete and self-accepting. Whatever happened to you was not your fault. It is crucial to forgive yourself. You can imagine the scenario in your head and change the way you have been dealt with. Turn the part you repressed to how you wanted it to happen, and give it a positive outcome. Bring it out to the light, see it as it is, and see the way it should have been.

Chapter 6

Trauma and the Formation of Core Beliefs

Core Beliefs

Core beliefs are deeply held, fundamental convictions about ourselves, others, and the world around us. They act as a mental framework or lens through which we interpret experiences and make sense of our lives. While some core beliefs are positive and contribute to a healthy self-image, others—especially those formed in response to trauma—can be harmful and limiting.

Formation of Core Beliefs:
   Core beliefs typically develop in childhood as we understand our environment and place within it. When these early influences are nurturing and supportive, we are more likely to create positive core beliefs, such as "I am lovable," "I am capable," and "I am safe." However, when a child is exposed to trauma, especially on a repeated or prolonged basis, the resulting core beliefs are often negative.

The Role of Trauma:
   Trauma can take many forms, including physical, emotional,

or sexual abuse, neglect, bullying, or even more subtle experiences like consistent invalidation of emotions or chronic exposure to conflict. When a child experiences trauma, they are often left feeling powerless, unsafe, and unworthy. These experiences can lead to the development of negative core beliefs that serve as a way for the child to make sense of what happened to them. For example, if a child is repeatedly neglected, they might develop the belief that "I am not important," which becomes a central part of their identity.

Common Negative Core Beliefs Stemming from Trauma

The core beliefs that arise from trauma are often deeply rooted in feelings of inadequacy, fear, and unworthiness. Some of the most common negative core beliefs include:

"I Am Unlovable":
This belief often forms in response to emotional neglect or rejection. A child who feels unloved or unwanted may internalize the assumption that they are inherently unlovable. This can lead to difficulties in forming and maintaining healthy relationships in adulthood, as the person may either avoid intimacy altogether or cling to unhealthy relationships to fill the void.

"I Am Not Safe":
Physical or emotional abuse, witnessing violence, or experiencing a chaotic environment can lead to the belief that the world is inherently dangerous and that safety is elusive. This belief can result in chronic anxiety, hypervigilance, and difficulties trusting others, as the individual constantly anticipates

harm or betrayal.

"I Am Not Good Enough":
This belief is common among individuals who experience constant criticism, high expectations, or failure to meet the standards set by caregivers or society. It can lead to a pervasive sense of inadequacy and a fear of failure, causing the individual to either overcompensate by striving for perfection or avoid challenges altogether to protect themselves from further feelings of inadequacy.

The Impact of Negative Core Beliefs on Life Choices

Negative core beliefs are not just passive thoughts; they shape how we interact with the world. These beliefs influence our behavior, relationships, and the opportunities we pursue (or avoid).

Behavioral Patterns:
When negative core beliefs go unchallenged, they often lead to maladaptive behaviors. For example, someone who believes "I am unlovable" might engage in self-sabotaging behaviors in relationships, such as pushing people away or clinging too tightly out of fear of abandonment. Similarly, people who believe "I am not good enough" might avoid growth opportunities altogether, such as promotions at work or pursuing personal goals, because they fear failure and rejection.

Self-Fulfilling Prophecy:
Negative core beliefs can create a self-fulfilling prophecy, where the belief itself leads to actions that reinforce it. For

instance, if you believe you are unworthy of love, you might unconsciously choose partners who are emotionally unavailable or abusive, thus strengthening your belief that you are unlovable. Over time, these repeated experiences can further entrench the negative belief, breaking free from the cycle even harder.

Influence on Relationships:

Relationships are often where negative core beliefs have the most profound impact. For example, someone who believes "I am not safe" may struggle with trust and intimacy, leading them to either isolate themselves or engage in relationships with controlling or abusive partners as a way to manage their fear. Alternatively, they may adopt a highly defensive or avoidant attachment style, pushing others away to protect themselves from potential harm.

Overcoming Negative Core Beliefs

The good news is that negative core beliefs, while deeply ingrained, are not immutable. With effort, awareness, and often professional support, it is possible to challenge and change these beliefs, leading to healthier behaviors and improved self-esteem.

Awareness and Acknowledgment:

The first step in overcoming negative core beliefs is to become aware of them. This involves recognizing the patterns in your thoughts and behaviors that stem from these beliefs. Do not be judgemental about these discoveries. You might feel disappointed when you mirror your core beliefs, but it is essential to forgive yourself for them. You are here to make a positive change. Don't beat yourself up over old beliefs; that will lead to self-sabotage. For example, if you notice that you consistently downplay your achievements or avoid social situations, this might be linked to a core belief that you are not good enough or that you are unlovable.

Challenging the Beliefs:

Once you've identified a negative core belief, the next step is to challenge it. This involves questioning the validity of the belief and gathering evidence to the contrary. For example, if you believe "I am unlovable," you might start by reflecting on the positive relationships in your life or the love and care you've received from others. Therapy, particularly cognitive-behavioral therapy (CBT), is often helpful in this process, as it provides tools and techniques for challenging and reframing negative beliefs.

Replacing Negative Beliefs with Positive Ones:

As you challenge your negative core beliefs, it is crucial to replace them with positive, more realistic ones. This might involve affirmations, journaling, or other practices reinforcing a healthier self-concept. For example, replacing "I am not good enough" with "I am capable and deserving of success" can gradually shift your mindset and lead to more positive outcomes in your life.

Building New Experiences:

Finally, building new experiences contradicting your negative core beliefs is crucial for lasting change. This might involve taking risks in relationships, pursuing new opportunities, or

CHAPTER 6

setting boundaries that affirm your self-worth. Over time, these positive experiences can help solidify new, healthier beliefs, allowing you to break free from the cycle of negativity and self-doubt.

Chapter 7

Positive self-supporting affirmations

You can write down these affirmations, say them out loud, or repeat them yourself.

I embrace who I am with love and compassion.

I accept my flaws because they make me unique.

I am enough just as I am.

I release the need to be perfect; I am perfectly imperfect.

Others' opinions of me do not define my worth.

I am valuable and deserving of love and respect.

My worth is inherent and does not depend on external validation.

I honor my needs and set healthy boundaries.

CHAPTER 7

I deserve good things, and I open my heart to receive them.

My dreams and desires are valid, and I am worthy of pursuing them.

I am my own best friend, treating myself with kindness and compassion.

I choose to love myself unconditionally, no matter what.

I nurture my body, mind, and soul with loving care.

I am proud of who I am becoming each day.

I celebrate my achievements, no matter how big or small.

I forgive myself for past mistakes; they are opportunities to learn and grow.

I release guilt and embrace self-compassion.

I am worthy of forgiveness, both from myself and others.

I let go of regret and focus on the present moment.

My past does not define me; I choose to live in the now.

I attract positivity and radiate it to others.

Every day is a fresh start, filled with new possibilities.

I control my happiness and choose to see the good in every situation.

My thoughts are powerful, and I choose those that uplift and empower me.

I am resilient, and I grow stronger with every challenge I face.

I choose to make conscious decisions in my life.

I chose love.

I forgive myself.

I am worthy.

I chose to create a conscious life.

I accept the consequences of my actions.

I make good choices.

People love me and respect me because I love and respect myself.

I radiate love and respect.

I am gentle to myself.

I am healing from my past and growing stronger every day.

CHAPTER 7

I release the pain from my past and embrace the love I deserve.

I am enough, and my feelings are valid.

I choose to be kind and compassionate to myself.

I accept myself fully, even when I work on my healing.

I chose to move forward in my life.

My emotions are real, and I tend to them.

I am dealing with my emotions and feelings.

I release other's negative energy.

I let go of past hurt feelings.

I can express my emotions safely.

I can feel the change when I am dealing with my past repressed emotions.

I contribute to my spiritual development by dealing with these past hurt feelings.

I elevate my spirit by forgiving myself.

I do the work.

How I change my attitude towards myself changes what kind

of people I attract into my life.

I can express myself freely.

People appreciate me.

I can change the course of my life by altering my beliefs.

I let my light shine.

I radiate love and acceptance.

I can rewrite my history.

Positive thoughts have a positive impact on me.

I am not what had happened to me; I am more than that.

I release all my past entanglements and create a clean slate for myself.

I grow in my personality every day.

I know where I am heading.

Chapter 8

Questions you can ask yourself to help you journalling and help you recall memories:

Uncover Painful Childhood Memories

What were my earliest memories of feeling scared, sad, or hurt? Who was involved, and how did I respond?

Have I ever felt like my needs were ignored or overlooked? What did I need that I didn't receive?

Can I remember a specific instance where I felt abandoned or alone? How did I cope with that feeling?

Were there moments when I felt unloved, unworthy, or rejected? What words or actions made me feel that way?

Did I ever feel like I had to hide parts of myself to gain love or approval? What were those parts, and who did I hide them from?

When did I first experience shame or guilt, and what caused those feelings? How did they shape my sense of self?

Were there times I was punished or criticized for expressing my true emotions? How did this affect my ability to express myself later in life?

Did I have to take on responsibilities too early in life? How did this impact my sense of safety and childhood innocence?

Questions to Identify Pain Points and Emotional Triggers

What situations in my current life make me feel small, powerless, or afraid? Can I trace these feelings back to similar experiences from my childhood?

Are there people or types of relationships that consistently trigger me? How do they remind me of people from my past?

What are my biggest fears, and where did they originate? Were there specific events or patterns in my childhood that planted these fears?

Do I struggle with trusting others? How might this relate to any broken trust or betrayal I experienced as a child?

In what ways do I still seek validation or approval from others? Does this need to connect with my lack of validation as a child?

When I get angry or upset, what age do I feel? Is there a younger version of myself trying to be heard or understood?

Are there any repetitive negative thoughts or beliefs I hold about myself? Where might these beliefs have originated in my childhood?

What do I wish someone had told me when I was a child? How would that have changed how I felt about myself or the world?

Questions to Foster Healing and Compassion for the Inner Child

What would I say or do if I could go back in time and comfort my younger self?

CHAPTER 8

What does my inner child need from me right now? How can I provide that comfort, safety, or love?

What activities or experiences made me feel truly happy and free as a child? How can I bring some of that joy into my life today?

How can I create a safe space for my inner child to express their feelings and fears? What would that look like in my daily life?

What kind of parent or guardian do I want to be for my inner child now? What loving, supportive behaviors can I adopt to show my inner child they are cared for?

References:

Exploring the path to lucidity – the dream interpretive. (2023, June 8). http://dreams-meanings-interpretations.com/2023/06/08/exploring-the-path-to-lucidity/

Minds, A. (2023, June 9). Not just shy or introverted: Understanding social anxiety. *AlignedMinds Therapy.* https://www.aligned-minds.com/post/breaking-free-from-social-anxiety

Pride, A., & Pride, A. (2024, August 20). *Ghost Mushrooms Review.* SetSet. https://thehigh.guide/psilocybin-to-explore-the-shadow-self/

Rand, G. G. (2023, April 16). *Mastering the Art of Daily Meditation: A guide to achieving mental, emotional, and spiritual balance | Gloria Rand.* Gloria Rand. https://gloriarand.com/mastering-the-art-of-daily-meditation-a-guide-to-achieving-mental-emotional-and-spiritual-balance/

Shah, P. F. (2023, June 18). *Shadow work: What is it? How can it help you heal?* Devi2Diva™. https://www.devi2diva.com/shadow-work-exercises/

Sophie. (2023, December 6). *Unlock the spiritual meaning of dreaming of fighting demons.* Inside My Dream. https://insidemydream.com/dream-of-fighting-demons-meaning/

SPECIALTIES | MySite. (n.d.). Mysite. https://www.attaining

REFERENCES:

clarity.com/specialties

Tiodar, A., & Tiodar, A. (2023, May 22). Shadow Work vs Light Work: This Is The Difference - Subconscious Servant. *Subconscious Servant - Mindfulness, Spirituality & Self-Care.* https://subconsciousservant.com/shadow-work-vs-light-work/

Also by Claire Sagy

You can learn how frequencies can heal you from this book:

Melody of Mindfulness: The Beginner's Guide to Sound Healing
-Just a glance into my book:
　-How do frequencies affect our body?
　-Is it a new thing?
　-Does it matter what kind of music I listen to?
　-How has the music industry kept us on a certain level?
　-What are the Chakra frequencies?
　-What are emotional frequencies?
　-Solfeggio frequencies
　-Healing frequencies

Milton Keynes UK
Ingram Content Group UK Ltd.
UKHW022002281124
451640UK00003B/9